A Little World Made Cunningly

A Little World Made Cunningly

GEORGE KLAWITTER

RESOURCE *Publications* • Eugene, Oregon

A LITTLE WORLD MADE CUNNINGLY

Copyright © 2024 George Klawitter. All rights reserved. Except for brief quotations in critical publications or reviews, no part of this book may be reproduced in any manner without prior written permission from the publisher. Write: Permissions, Wipf and Stock Publishers, 199 W. 8th Ave., Suite 3, Eugene, OR 97401.

Resource Publications
An Imprint of Wipf and Stock Publishers
199 W. 8th Ave., Suite 3
Eugene, OR 97401

www.wipfandstock.com

PAPERBACK ISBN: 979-8-3852-1205-7
HARDCOVER ISBN: 979-8-3852-1206-4
EBOOK ISBN: 979-8-3852-1207-1

for Susan

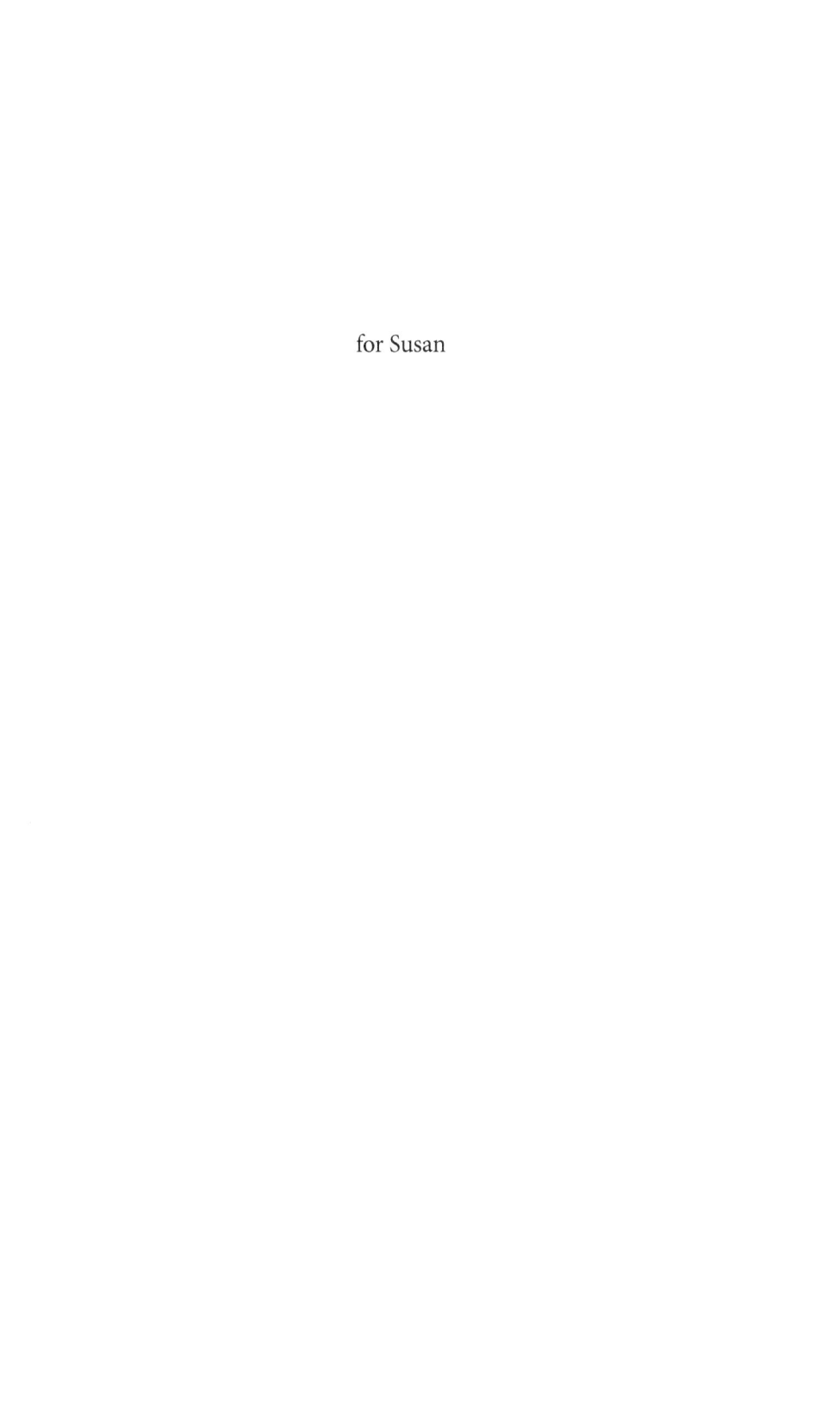

The burial shroud has no pockets.
 —Pope Francis

Senior Biology at Clifton High

Darwin? Just a name
to farmer kids high on Jesus,
so the very thought they came from
bonobos brings fits of laughter

ricocheting up the musty rows
to old Miss Prism, pencil smart
and angular like a marble ruler,
who never blinks but flips

the lights back on, smooths
her auburn hair and smiles,
"That'll be enough today—
remember the report for Thursday."

As her urchins scramble for the door,
thoughts of each other
locked in country love
seep from their born-again brains.

The room's projector whirs its sigh
to STOP, and the emptiness
of desks stack up inside
their teacher's mind.

She gathers scribbled things,
a forgotten comb, a crumpled love-note,
and waltzes down to the teachers' lounge
for a smoke and a bit of gossip.

My Clifton Church

Convinced the world is evil, I tell
my people they can be saved
from nameless fear and certain fate

if they will harken to my light,
the kind that pierces from my eyeballs
into their blackened Texas souls,

if the ladies will arm themselves
with shotguns to preserve their bodies
for their randy rancher husbands,

if their children will drop their smiles
and turn unto the Lord for righteousness,
dropping easy hopes for dense uncertainties,

if they sing loud enough to blast
the heavens where our Savior sits
in radiant judgment ready to strike,

if they take my truth as theirs,
admit no other and beat themselves
into submission to the Lamb.

Then all will be well, and the light
will shine on Clifton, each home
ablaze with love for each—and God of course.

Alma

I had an old neighbor—
she died at a hundred and four—
who thrilled to savor
all the things I planted out-of-doors.

I'd put in a Lady Baltimore—
she'd hint that she'd like one.
I'd put in a tomato plant or pour
petunias into the sun—

she'd suggest that some
would look nice in her front yard.
So our gardens grew dumb,
quiet with crinkly Swiss chard.

She'd sit in an old plastic chair
out of the light to read
her ladies' magazines, her hair
immaculate under curlers. Indeed.

She'd watch my flowers grow
taller than hers but never
let an unkind word go
between us, not once, not ever.

Eventually she died, was buried
in the dusty Texas dirt,
her DNA married
to roots of things inert.

I wait to see her rise in buttercups
or a passion vine to run along
the sidewalk where delivery trucks
won't mash it. Like a song

gone berserk she twists my mind
into a tangle of elephant grass.
I long for color—she gives me bland
grays and browns that pass

for color. But I understand
and let her enjoy the sun.
I do, even as I rake the land,
hum her tune, see us two for two.

Trojan Man

I can't think of Troy without seeing him
on battlements gone to grass,
standing at the massive trench that Schliemann
ripped into the northern wall.

He frowns, I frown—he smiles, I smile.
I have no life in Troy aside from his.
My eyes assume his eyes
at every stone he trembles into dust.

I wince and wonder where is Hector?
Priam too and archer Paris?
All my heroes fallen in the trash of Troy,
here where the wind never stops

and menacing ships from Sparta dock,
display their tense marauders,
and wait for Zeus to let them in the gates,
cowards all, down to brash Odysseus,

the cuckold Menelaus, and the most supreme
of egoists, Agamemnon of the thousand lies.
Achilles too will get his own someday—
when Virgil's done with him he'll howl

his fate inside some barren afterlife
where nothing moves outside of time
and fallen heroes mesh with fallen traitors
awash in stupid hapless glory

turned to ashes. In their deadened throats
where's the hubris now,
the love of battle,
aristeia waiting in the wings?

Everything is dirt and weeds at Troy,
the only glint of Ares and Athena
the summer's wild flowers laughing in the sun,
the only glories left from deathless Ilium.

Her Ground Time Here was Brief

for Maxine Kumin
February 6, 2014

It's snowing again
through the furry needles
of the crusty pine.

We see the slivers dropping
white, more white, more white,
on the cars and parking lot.

At dusk a swan lifts
off the lake, tries to navigate
our roof, but drops.

The dark obscures her thud,
her fall outside the upper window
to the glassy grass below.

Poor thing. She'll lie beneath
the drifts until the spring
unseals her broken body.

Then we'll shovel her stubborn
feathers into the dumpster,
and sing a song for Kumin,
also gone this solemn winter night.

In Memory of Gregory Corso

I like to think he's sitting here
in an upholstered armchair day by day
spinning stories in his deathless brain,
waiting for his ghosts to resurrect.

He used to wander Denver streets,
rummaging in garbage cans for sandwich-ends,
pearls in the bottom of amber bottles.
He'd wait on street corners for the light to change.

Now he slumps in New York somewhere
in his daughter's house. She feeds him
like a marmoset and brings him magazines
he doesn't read. When he asks for paper and pen,

she brings them knowing nothing will come petering
out of that desiccated mind long ago emptied
of every dancing metaphor and burning thought.
The pen will be uncapped and papers dropped.

When visitors knock, she discourages them,
frisking them for pills and cans and bottles.
Her dad is a recovering something
so nothing foreign can pollute his blood.

He dreams self back to beavered times
when he roamed the stage with Kerouac, Cassidy,
and that high priest of cult, Ginsberg.
All gone. Only Peter stays to stoke the flame.

Gregory knows nothing of their grand success
because the crumbs of notoriety he could scavenge
never brought him much to live for, even
though his impish beauty made him our dream-boy.

Sure Kerouac was prettier, but beauty froze
in Jack with manhood. Little Gregory never
felt the thaw of boyish charm—as he slipped
into oblivion, floating back to hippier days.

What Museums Do for Us

Yes, I've been to the Louvre.
Funny you should ask,
not that I'd throw it in your face

the way they do in travel mags
or slip it in between your sushi bites
at chichi cocktail parties.

Flandrin was my favorite,
but obviously not for the curator
or the hordes who passed beneath it.

There—high up on the wall,
one among a hundred in that room
of gilded frames and oil paint.

He's hunched, nude of course,
seaside, with the ache of the world
crushing his head to his knees,

oblivious of the dark sky,
the impending gloom of a storm,
the thunder out over the sea.

His girlfriend dumped him,
or his boyfriend—maybe both
ran off together into sunlight,

laughing among the frilly butterflies,
the Shasta daisies bobbing
along the path to sexual fulfillment.

So here he crouches, the mirror of our psyche,
waiting for a touch on his saddened shoulder,
his earnest hope we'll understand.

I'll let him know the futility of dreams,
of expectations, and yes, of love
that poses Flandrin-style on rocks,

seaside, naked, very much out of love,
but available, ever available,
for a kiss toward resurrection.

The Cubist Game

His football brain runs a play
the way Picasso ran a painting—
you never know just where a squiggle
will become a running back.

Out of nowhere a line breaks open,
the guards no longer right or left,
so where you might expect an arc,
you get a dash with blur of color.

Then when the jumble rearranges in
your mind some mauve remembered thing,
you breathe a shout because your man
stands resurrected underneath the post.

You never realized how painterly he is
until the movement's finalized,
the brushstrokes gathered to a masterpiece:
Imagination on a Field of Green.

No, it's not for sale. If you want
the thrill of huddle, thrust, and tackle,
paint your own—nine hunky men
in yellow tights dancing on a canvas.

Throw the ball in tempera, oil, acrylic,
and let the palette soften it to moonbeam
on the yard lines. Then pack up your brushes,
hit the showers, wait for replay, live for dreams.

Memories Are Made

Old Route 30 was a sometime thrill,
heading east out of our prairie town
through the likes of Dyer and Valpo,
new sights out every window.

We were good because we had to be,
scared beyond regret by mystery,
watching the corn unwind in August,
the wheat shimmer in a sudden gust,

my father at the wheel, my mother
clutching a purse and musing,
three of us in the back seat
scrapping over this or that.

Once on an off-road we had taken
to reach a family reunion we didn't
particularly want to attend,
we saw something we didn't want to see—

a bicycle, small not large,
crumpled under a bloody sheet,
one shoed leg sticking out for
slowing cars to gawk at.

Some things are seared into memory.
For me forever that summer shock,
wonder ever after: was it boy or girl?
red hair or brown? freckled or not?

We passed in silence,
our five-second eternity pasted
under the summer sun, a part
of us, never to be forgotten.

And the perp nowhere to be seen,
off somewhere with the radio blaring
to mask the scene on an endless loop
in his hamster-on-a-wheel brain.

Annual Torture

Piano recitals at Miss Brown's—
sixteen students on the program,
and you have to sit through three
murdering "Twinkle, Twinkle"

and two destroying "Für Elise"
before you get to a little Liszt
or a touch of Chopin.

It's almost not worth the punch
or lace magnolia cookies
year after year.

But we'll be back again,
circling like barnyard fowl,
waiting for the death of Beethoven,
children torturing Bach.

The dead guys never stop
the joy of giving, even if it's only
a pleasant chord here and there.

Some years Miss Brown herself
ascends the bench and gives
her soul to Debussy or Mendelssohn.

Her bantam nose sometimes anoints
the keys, cautiously caught up
in the dizzy spell of magic,
a sudden splash of pianissimo.

One year she shocked us
with a swift glissando.
No one expected that—
or her sly smile.

The Anesthesiologists

for Matthew Coscia

While we're asleep, they assume our lives,
assimilating charts and screens,
manipulating drips of red and grey.

As we drift bottomless, they rock
the tubes that lull us to and fro,
making much of blips and lines.

To work their magic best they need our souls,
and so they study all our data
while the knife and laser probe.

From the table a ballerina becomes
a dancer in a mask white with gauze,
tapping toes on hospital terrazzo.

A philosopher strapped for surgery
oozes into those who'll slash for Plato,
snipping bits of rhetoric, quibbling over fact.

An ancient virgin drowsing into vision
doesn't sense the gowned ones shaming lust,
three tense hours tamed by vow and prayer.

So steady mime and apery shape their task,
not easy in the antic filigree of a child
or the brittle parchment of a racist clown.

Today a socialite, tomorrow homeless joe,
always on the prowl for similitude:
a bloated banker, quarterback, or summer acrobat.

All Protean-slithered into operation roles,
squirm and pirouette, catching passes in the end zone,
cooking cordon bleu, just this side of sweet eternity.

Candle in the Snow

Our local Buddhist Bernie
trudges every day out into the snow
to fix a lighted candle in a box
atop a rock where it shines
throughout the night to tell us something.

I'm not sure what. Everything
he does is mystery as he slims
his way around the house tan
as a mouse and lithe. He locks
his heart outside our minds.

No matter. When he climbs
the hill back through the yard swinging
helter-skelter, tossing whims
we look for, he's the man
we reverence shirt to socks.

If uncertainty knocks,
he answers with his antic grin,
like as not also singing
some recent chapel hymn
in tune as best he can.

Why then when he ran
out of life were we shocked,
we who honored him,
we who stood thrilling
for his antique kith and kin?

Like Mother, Like Son

Paul Verlaine's saintly mother
kept her still-born babies pickled,
two of them, in her Paris bedroom where
their glass jars swam in winter sun.

Her drunken son, the spoiled sotty poet,
high on absinthe, pride, and God knows what,
smashed his siblings out one afternoon,
smeared their fetal guts into the rug.

Mme. Verlaine wrote no poems to let
us know her feelings about her rabid son,
but her velvet dresses gourmandized
formaldehyde hem to hem

as she swished her way through religion,
politics, and stupor, propping up
her boy. He clawed his way with
rhyme debris, counting syllables.

If his mother wept, we'll never know.
Meanwhile the poet greased his solo way
to notoriety, his alexandrines
peppering the café bums who sat

night after night stoking each other's ego,
condemning ordinary folk who simply
craved a little warmth, a little light
to pull them through another day to death.

Evenings his little fuck-baby Rimbaud
scrawled poems with his own godly feces
on a tabletop in the Café des Deux Magots
for sweet Verlaine. Both graze into eternity.

The End of the Beginning

Your going wasn't mixed with tears. My fear
we wouldn't meet again evaporated
when you told me every time I thought
of you, you'd resurrect inside my heart.

I never really thought we'd be apart,
but to both of us it was pretty clear
we couldn't really call when separated
or sing as one the joys that summer brought.

Was it you or was it I who taught
the other one the only way to start
fraternal love, the love we thought so dear,
was to see our sins eradicated?

Once we knew our love was indicated
in the stars, we never quarreled or fought—
even as you slipped into the dark,
your going void of senseless, wanton fear.

War and Hell

Never for me the pulse of war,
never the decision to, YES SIR,
follow a corporal to the front
with my rifle tight in my sweaty hands,

never the glare of fire overhead,
never the stench of smoke and rot,
no brambles to push through,

no swamp to slosh through,
waist high in murk,
afraid of snakes and who knows what,

no god but the god of fear
and only the thought of you inside me.

But I have made decisions, have followed counsel
sometimes, and leapt for a train at the last second,
deciding in the winter night to go,

not stay in the warmth of stasis,
opted for the unknown, even the unknowable,

when the plash of bodies in cassocks
prone on the sanctuary marble
boasted all the same vows
to the same unforgiving future,

fought for the right to be abused
in chalky classrooms in various cities,
washed by some dream
that it all made sense or would some day

on a porch rocking,
surrounded by a lifetime
of maybe and no
and the absolute glow of evening.

Boy

One Sunday morning after church
I went out the wrong door.
The world caved in.

I was lost.
No matter that God lived there.
I was afraid of everything:

the cavernous garages
where the priests parked their cars,
the tall oaks with leaves

that never stopped rustling,
the locked school.
Nothing made sense.

Some lady said,
"He wants his Mommy."
Just like that.

Then my father came around
the back side of the church
and took my hand.

I don't remember anything
earlier from my childhood.
Or was this yesterday?

The Writer

He comes out for a visit
now and then

but most of the time
he's in his chambered nautilus

translating life
into words.

The Pair

on a painting by Ruth Ortiz

He and the boat are fused—
connected by a thread
from the pond to his little finger,

far from his orchid mother,
in a forest washed
with honeydew.

Happy to be tethered,
the boat sings
as the urchin walks the lupine path

coaxing now and then
his pet to follow,
white sails on a red mast.

Outing

for Ed Condon

In Ireland the Blarney stone still weeps
against the odor of the sea, and Irish grass
creeps up foundations of somebody's castle,
waits to be dried for fuel in a stove.

No matter that I held your legs as you
leaned out beneath the grey-cold stones—
behind each stone an angel unafraid
to brace its fingers in the settled clay.

You're free, no longer in the wicker cage
the world weaves. A wider universe
accepts you for its own, refuses categories,
lets you play among the stars unmarked.

Your baby soul races with the seraphim
at tinker toys beside the emerald throne.
No one remembers you were slated for mortality
so winsome is your smile, so gentle are your eyes.

Country Visit

Nude he is as delicate as a fawn.
Moving along the path from house to pool,
he waits for guests to satisfy his mood,
stir the summer water, taste the wind.

Nothing for his visitors can hint
of impropriety: the wine, the food,
must be as perfect as a Persian jewel,
as flawless as an unvoiced Schubert song.

They come. They eat. They swim. They rave. They're gone.
Then he dusts the Chinese paintings where the cruel
stares of dilettantes had settled, the rosewood
begging polish where greasy fingers sinned.

By early evening sprays of mint
will balm the air where urban misfits stood.
Cleanliness remains his silvan tool,
his only text *l'après-midi d'un faun.*

Danseur

He's as quiet as a valley, yet
a river of good humor passes through
his soul, surprises you, enchanted, sweet.
So when you walk along his silver grass,

he pirouettes and lands, a laughing jet
of blue in front of you. No arabesque
was ever cut so pure, an honor due
from gods to feet of wind and back of steel.

This gift from heaven comforts as his body
weaves hosannas here among the crass
and crabbed, a grand surprise from up above,

dropped from nectar-dripping clouds, hardy,
boned and muscled. Each plié suggests
no wonder known or waited for but love.

Taylor Out of Ron

for Ron Cabal

Son of a shaman, he should have known
he'd charm the trees. You heard him once
in an angry wind—that way he had
of strutting like a bandy rooster,

the cock-o-the-walk. Then he'd show
a smile as wide of joy as fun,
a mixture of the good and bad
that blended in his bouncy blues step.

His guitar and he were best of friends—
they bonded. And when he closed his eyes
in song, you knew you'd lost him. Someone
on a cloud somewhere had him.

He touched where he went, but lightly. When
he left, you knew you missed a prize—
his way of saying "bye," a come-on
trailing back, never dark or dim.

The Darker Side of Camelot

for Chris Flynn

The yard already a mystery goblin-style
with bushy corners dark and unexplored,
raccoons in love tumbling around,
fumbling for bits of apple and bread
the owner jettisoned out the back door,

dank magnolia trees, their black-green
rustling under a heavy sky
no one ever sees, the only light
a string of multi-colored Christmas bulbs
beading their way across the broken eaves.

Driving by, no one ever knows what
to expect—some poppets in the dirt,
some half attempt at geranium dying
in the Texas heat, their faces red
upturned to despair and ruin,

of course a big smelly dog nosing
in the broken shards of yesteryear.
Now the colonel's putting up a fence, tin,
galvanized, like the kind a concentration camp
would love, the posts secure against escape.

Next, no doubt, some curled electric wire
and searchlights activated by a flea.
They'll be on all night illuminating
rows of guinea pigs lined up for roll,
squealing for a little milk or soup.

Some men have hobbies—
playing dominoes, collecting stamps—
this man's obsessed with privacy
yet says, "Would you like to come
and play in my backyard?"

Once in, you're his, and the fingernails
you once enjoyed will join a heap
along with whatever teeth he fancies
and your balls, of course, needed
for the feast of Hallows Eve.

So avoid the hell, move on,
let the neighbor kids inspire
his torture den, bloodied whips,
the kind that keeps some coming back,
ever on the prowl for thrill and fear.

I was there once and survived—
just barely. Now it's retrospect
for me, the agony of knowing I was there,
escaped, lived to warn the wary,
lure the fools away from ecstasy.

Photographer

for Arlen

Some may be able to tell where his eye
ends and the camera begins—I can't.
White flame shoots out, time freezes
in an ice of instant, the richer for his smile

over muscle, over brawn, the cry
of landscape, city, water, and the rant
that traffic brings. All things fast he teases
into moment. Clashing red and green beguile

to mauve inside his gentle, artful brain
where angels rearrange realities,
resolve disgrace, absolve the sin that shame

smears into time. The wild relaxes tame,
sweetness flowering sepia—he sees
through mist the sun that follows rain.

The Cellists

for David Sandelin

It had to happen. When the cellists play
across the living room, the vision shatters
that old dream the years had fostered through
a fog of law and tort. Your smile reflects

from iris vase to snowdrop, and the day
breaks through the window as if it matters.
What was old submits to what is new,
a revelation only time suspects

because you change, I change, we change. So few
the hours left before eternity
converts our flesh to dew, our bone to ash.

I'll never claim a single thing of you
but cold respect, a light fraternity,
a simple joy that tightens as we pass.

Glass Blower

With fingers delicate as spider legs
he hands the rod into the waiting flame
and watches as the glass transforms into
a joy of color dancing underneath

his eyes. It resonates when he begs
his breath gently down the tube the same
as if in Eden he'd coaxed Adam through
a flesh and bone silicone sheath.

I take my treasure home but never wash
it since his touches on the vase remain
sweet tinctures swimming in the winter light:

he's on the shelf radiating gouache,
pastel, acrylic, oil, and sand to frame
my thrilling soul today with wild night.

Ye Olde Rock & Roll

He jumped at the piano, beating
keys with both his hammy fists,
screaming, "Great Balls of Fire!"

Of course, we loved him, even
when he married that little girl.
How could we not revere him?

He nourished our blood, got
our juices flowing, said what
we wanted to say but couldn't.

No matter. He's dead now,
untamed but dead. We loved
all those slammered notes.

But so much better to fade like Fats
off Blueberry Hill into the muck
Katrina did to his Lower 9th house.

And that pink Cadillac in his
front yard—did it squirm
with jellyfish from the hurricane?

Fats our man, the whole ton of him.
That sweet, sweet voice telling us
where he found his thrill.

Our blood cool, we love him
in our antique days. Except
on those brash occasions

when our heart pumps for Jerry,
and we spin his platters
to get our hormones shaking.

The Wreck of the Livonia

*Whereby Thirteen Felician Nuns Died
of the Covid Virus in One Month, 2020*

The sweetness of the convent—
the gentle rhyme of mother
come and then of mother sent,
syllables heavenward bother,
obedience ever never cross or blind,
a swoop of angel wing to sing another
born of simple maid assigned
a sign of rapture quieted, whispered, meant.

The thirteen virgins
there in Michigan,
where rivers teem in steely sturgeon,
a wisp of horror begun
by stealth serves the lips' *Magnificat*,
spins out in viral terror, hellish spun,
pinched pandemic-bright to rot
the lungs in vivid shreds, devilled sickly version.

No use to hide
behind the saintly names,
the lost librarian, the ride
of Covid over dames
made holy throughout years of welcomed pain
embraced for Jesus, statutory claims
of virtue polished to a vein
divine of heaven-scent from His sacred side.

Good Friday takes
the first two, quick to go,
the nails fresh, the crown from stakes
of briar, broken glow

for voyaging beyond the hurt of hurt,
the shame of crucifixion, painful, slow,
and capillaries pert-alert,
a soothing glide, the subtle nervous quakes.

Good-by, each Mary
of the precious thirteen—
Luiza, Celine, Estelle, the very
joy of Thomas, unseen
Patricia, Clarence, Rose, and Janice, culled
for Paradise with Alice Ann, careen
into Martinez, undulled
Victoria, and Madeleine in song, and carry

(last to go)
Donathan along—
she waited months, and so
discipleship's complete in song
of cherubim and precious jeweled thrones
around the holy face—no right, no wrong,
no dense Livonian sickbed moans—
just God, Her loving light, Felician-sweet, to know

we worship you
through Him as you can fuse
now glorified, vibrant, true
to tense but wondrous news:
you're Him, He's you, combination green,
no aged limbs, you've paid purgation's dues,
relaxed inside seraphic scene
gone to rainbow rose, empurpled gold, and blue.

First Mass

for Andrew Fritz, CSC

The first time that you transubstantiate
I'll be there in a quiet, subtle pew
watching you, your fingers on the bread,
your breath across the chaliced purple wine,

the angels singing as you consecrate,
the holy words enfeebled from your lips. You
'll be lost in love, the grace of state instead
outside you in the bread and wine, the sign.

Warm reds and blues will filter from the paned
stained glass along the walls on either side,
and incense rich with spice will filter up.

You'll be no longer you, but golden veined
with sweet divinity, the Spirit pied
across your soul, soft eyes, the dish, the cup.

A Little World Made Cunningly

Hollyhocks never grew in her garden
but stayed her alley flower.
Yet how we loved their scratchy poles

on hot August days sprouting trumpets
pink and lavender and white, each with
a dusty yellow tongue fumbled by bumblebees.

If my grandmother noticed those stacks of flowers,
she never said so as she poked among
her precious vegetable and berry patches.

But what would the alley be without her sentinels?
A scary place for grandchildren, the lesser for a lack
of color, music, light, and garden culture.

They died each autumn,
gone to hard brown pods encircling seeds,
rough to our touch and sight,

the stalks bending under cold rain,
dropping hopeful disks to musty loam,
looking through the winter into spring.

Brown and Green

My grandmother lived with nature
alongside a house, a big one in fact,
with a parlor no one ever used
and a screened-in porch (home to spiders),
and a bathroom of sorts, an after-thought.

Her heart was out-of-doors,
first in the spring when the purple iris
triumphed with gold along the south side
of the brown-shingled house,
waiting for the morning sun,

the lilies-of-the-valley in the shade,
the ominous dark under the porch,
lilies with a heavy scent, heavy
for so slight a waxy bell of a flower,
almost gone before you found them,

the apple trees all in a row,
their white clusters blooming
against the push of the wind,
shaking boughs against the Midwest sky,
dropping sweet petals to the grass below,

the twisted pear, sleepy
above the asparagus patch,
the ghostly apricot, oriental, quaint,
facing two cherry trees waiting their turn
for sunshine and April rain,

the rhubarb thick with elephant leaves
and ruddy stems, guarding the corner
behind the blackberry patch we never entered
because the prickles and thorns
were sure to draw blood,

elderberry too—how she watched
the lacy blooms turn to purple fruit
and managed to save them from the birds
who wanted their fill
of the garden so potent in summer,

all semi-wild, hanging as everything did,
on the edge of an empty lot
transformed into her vegetable plot
after the rains relaxed and allowed
her out into the fresh-turned dirt.

There the corn arose in quiet stalks,
and cucumbers ran their frilly vines
into the pepper spot. The tomatoes
sang into the sun while her watchful fingers
snagged the chartreuse worms away.

Rutabaga, onion, pole beans—
all spilling into the August heat.
One year even celery, a gentle crop
along the boards that snaked a path
through the occasional mud.

She thrived in this world of brown and green,
happiest on her knees in the dirt,
coaxing the weak, weeding the choked,
gathering an apron of ground-cherries
in their paper-thin Chinese lantern shells.

Could she have lived in the garden
she would have, among the bumblebees
and summer critters. There was her heart,
nurturing something every day,
more a part of the garden than of us.

Grandmother's Kitchen

Small but warm
with one window
looking into the garden.

A stove that cooked
anything she harvested
summer and fall.

A husband who ate
anything she made.
He rarely talked.

That kitchen came alive
December 6 every year
when Old St. Nick appeared—

or rather didn't.

All the grandchildren
crowding around the table
waiting for the THUD

from the unheated back bedroom
where the window was left open
for Old Nick (Uncle Bob) to fling

a gunny sack of oranges,
apples, nuts, and candy
onto the hardwood floor.

The excitement grew
as Grandma doled a share
of the evening's goodies

to each expecting child.

Springerle

When my grandmother mixed her dough
for springerle every Christmas,
I never understood her abiding sadness,

but there it was, as palpable
as the anise in the air
hanging above her special mixing bowl.

Then when the cookies rested overnight
in the darkness of the cold back porch
away from joy and German hands

to frost themselves in mystery
with caps so crunchy white
you'd think the angels touched them,

I'd sense the wonder of the process
and know somehow the pain she had
with her husband laughing across town

in his other lady's kitchen
where no cookies squirmed into the dark
as he fondled her across his ancient knees.

What if she never baked them?
What if they stayed forever on their colding sheets
as December snows came and went?

What if the knowledge of life so
overwhelmed her that the cookies
never came to oven grandeur

but stayed a stupid possibility
out there, far from the bite
of adolescent teeth on Christmas Eve?

The Gardener

My father's German hands were gentle.
He planted baby's breath each summer
to line the sidewalk from our front door
down the pebbled driveway to the street.

I don't know why he was so careful in his ministry—
we lived on a dead-end so no one passed in transit,
and the neighbors had their own screaming lives
to bother them away from summer flowers.

He may have done it for my mother, but she
to my recollection never said "how pretty"
and never clipped his lilacs or his peonies
for a crystal vase on the dining room table.

Perhaps he cultivated beauty for himself,
that hidden self his children never saw but felt
as it trickled out in blossoms under fingers
meant for other things: business talk and baseball.

Diamond Wire & Cable, Inc.

When my mother went to work at age fifteen
at a lamp factory in Chicago Heights,
she never complained.

She earned nine cents an hour,
ten hours a day, six days a week,
$5.40 her take-home pay every Saturday.

Working on lamp cords to feed a conveyor belt,
she didn't get paid if the machine broke down.
But she accepted what she got in "The Depression."

She never sat down, all day.
The acid bath for the extension cords ate
at her skinny teen-age fingers.

At 21 she married my father who said,
"No wife of mine is going to work in a factory."
She said it was the happiest day in her life.

Mercury Poisoning

My mother lightninged into the living-room
when she heard the crash of metal on glass.
It wasn't like her to move that fast—
her usual gait more suited to a tomb.

But there she was, abuzz with rectitude,
surveying the mess my brother and I had made
reaching for the phial of mercury my dad
kept on a top shelf in dad-solicitude.

We'd played with it before, letting the gray beads
roll between our fingers and wondering if
the stuff was ever hard or stiff—
so odd to taste on our tongue seeds.

We never realized the junk was poison
or a cure for syphilis (what's that?) or
a magic snake creeping up the skinny core
of a simple bland thermometer. So noisome.

Then the wonder came rushing down on us,
we two boys in the debris of broken shelves.
We could blame no one but ourselves
as we waited for the gathering fuss—

which didn't come. I think a mother's heart
outweighs her brain ounce for ounce.
At least hers did. She didn't pounce
to threaten discipline. For her part

she was glad we were alive and ignorant
perhaps as we were what mercury could do
to the stomachs of a boy. She knew
we were still alive, less or more intelligent.

Aunt Rosella Theodora

A beautician by wish and talent,
she spent her life prettifying others:
neighbor ladies, sisters, daughters.

They came to her bedraggled
so she frimped and puffed them
into movie star celebrities,

each "do" a work of art,
a wonder for the world of Steger
where she plied her basement trade.

No head too mean, no hair too wiry—
she blessed them all with soaps and creams,
and put them under air to incubate.

Voila! another masterpiece greets the sun
while goddesses above are pouting
they never waxen under sweet Rosella's hands.

Later she slips into her garden
where begonia red and yellow wait their turn,
and nasturtium smiling in Technicolor.

She tweaks them with the same dear motherness
she gives to ladies. Bouffant or petal—
all the same in a day's careful rites.

Great-Aunt Agnes

She ran the place with an iron tongue—
that immaculate farm on a Wisconsin county road.
She had eight boys—no girls—and a husband,
my Uncle Al, who never talked but knew how to listen.

And how to work—they all worked under the lash
of that iron tongue. She knew the value of money,
having inherited a bundle from the sale
of the North Dakota farm her step-father owned.

Well, not really her step-father—she was strong about that—
she never took his name and resented his memory
but not his money, which got her a quiet husband
and a farm that ran like a well-oiled combine.

She had those eight boys working dawn to dusk,
each one allotted chores to learn responsibility
and the need for money—lots of it—and no complaints—
it was the way of the world and she ruled it.

Of course, their reward was manicured sex
they learned by watching the animals in their care.
Every day they saw what animals enjoyed,
those critters fattening for the family knife.

The pigs, the cows, the chickens—all climbing
while the boys supervised and learned the need
to channel energy into glorious minutes,
summer, winter, year-round with local farm girls.

The oldest boy went off to the Dominicans.
His father cried the whole drive up to Minnesota,
probably over the loss of two hands on the farm
to help lighten the noise from the wife.

Great-uncle Al cried the whole damn ride
and dropped the boy off to the monks
with their curious celibacy that nobody understood,
least of all the ones who supposedly practiced it.

Then the truck pulled back to the Beloit farm,
the seven remaining boys learning to survive,
with the termagant who barked the orders:
never to be crossed or punishment would follow.

What a world! But my family envied that world:
the order, the discipline, the manicured yard,
the obedient animals, the money pouring in,
and everyone Republican, terse, pitchfork in hand.

I wonder today if all the boys have thrived—
dementia, I'm told, rampant in their aging brains.
Old Mama Nature got the best of them
or what was left behind from Mama Agnes.

Did Agnes have a soft side after all? The dog—
she always had a dachshund, worthless,
that couldn't be fattened for a valuable kill,
that never did a lick of work around the place.

Maybe Agnes liked the sight of something
totally unlike herself, something that never worked,
not one single minute of the day,
just waddled around the farmhouse, content to eat and sleep,

things the mistress didn't have much time for,
not with the need to raise those eight gorgeous boys,
prime them for the marriage market, rein in
their adolescent cares, channel everything to family.

She's buried in the churchyard with her husband.
Quiet as ever, he does as he's told
while she schemes out their new lives under snow
and Wisconsin sun, things she never could control.

Aunt Tillie

My sweet Aunt Tillie never used
her real name—Matilda.
Even for her tombstone she
insisted on "Tillie," just "Tillie."

Lady farmer, she hated watermelon
and blueberries. Honey too—
she called it "bee spit,"
in German, of course.

After her only son moved
to California with his new wife,
she stayed behind, always the grateful lady,
in our little Illinois town.

She beat breast cancer in her 30's.
Her sister Sophie didn't—and died.
Then Tillie in her 80's one morning
fell down the basement stairs,

fractured her pelvis
and couldn't stand.
She crawled back up
to the kitchen for the phone.

But she couldn't reach it,
high up as it was
on the yellow kitchen wall
between two plastic roosters.

She tried all day flipping
the telephone cord. At last
the phone fell down to her
and she dialed for help.

Off to the hospital,
then back home alone,
the cancer returning
to her sweet nothing body.

Dr. Armbruster said
that sometimes happens—
trauma can trigger
old sleepy cancer cells.

They moved her to California
with a few of her antiques
to live with her only son
in the sunshine.

I saw her only once after that,
the saddest woman alive,
incapable of cheer,
sweet Aunt Tillie.

Now when I visit her grave,
I see that name on the stone,
and "Tillie" haunts me
in daylight dreams.

Students

I give all of them my life,
and they give me their colds
and flu and once pneumonia.

They cough, they wheeze, they sneeze
on everything, mostly on me,
their local handkerchief.

Some of them, I think,
would like to give me herpes
and subtle gonorrhea.

But they settle for some strep,
bronchitis now and then,
an ague and a chill.

Someday they'll give me cancer,
a heart attack, or stroke,
always knowing it's better to give
than to receive.

Hockey Duo

When I told him that I saw
his girl waltzing down the corridor
with the campus quarterback,

he just smiled that sly
koala-bear smile at me,
then went back to chewing eucalyptus:

he knew a silver-tongued puck
when he saw one, his heart
knowing what it always knew.

Then his buddy told me
their roommate got thirteen teeth
smashed out by some Cro-Magnon icer.

The rink can be a brutal place,
an alligator whirl of twisting bodies,
sticks slicing air and ears.

Yes, I'll be back next season
watching from the heated stands,
waiting for the clash and blood,

watching both of them fight
when I'd rather see them fixing
pentameter in their latest sonnet.

Crew

for Jack Westner and Patrick Armstrong

Galley slaves, they row until their hands
are fused into the oars, one with wood,
taut with pull and pull, no relaxation
from the strain, except the moment's lull

before the pull, virgin-loose, man for man,
against the water and the coxswain's word
PULL, the rabid run of recreation
gone to work, enslaved, sold for fun.

But aren't their brains working sweet, stanzaic,
as the lashes on their backs cut deep?
Aren't they creating poems in their mind?

The master's whip can't make their souls prosaic.
No! The syllables rub through their sleep
to blossom sonnets, ballads, soft, refined.

Rugby

I go to see a game I don't
understand. I go because
my freshmen are playing.

Men in green rushing
to and fro, pushing as if eager
to get to the front of something.

I see Jack make what looks
like a touchdown—he's rolling
on the ground across a white line.

I want to shout "Hurray!"
but nobody else is shouting, and
the players aren't stopping.

I don't have a clue what's
happening. Daniel is nowhere
in sight. Maybe he quit.

Now they're in a big circle
bent over in half, shoving
each other for some reason.

The white ball appears from nowhere
and everyone is grabbing.
It tries to get away.

Then everyone is hurtling down field
and nothing makes sense.
Every act is a blur.

Thank heavens for the blue sky,
and the cold green grass,
and a soft September breeze.

Hints of autumn are in the air.
The geese have left the lake.
Not a firefly in sight.

Hibernation is coming. Maybe
these men too will settle
in some cave for the winter.

For a Student

As quiet as a rainbow,
he appears weekly in my classroom,
sits, and waits in color for instruction.

I feed him poetry. He listens
politely, marmoset-fashion,
then leaves, no helmet for his head.

Mister Invulnerable!
Rainbows are like that—
they effervesce at will, eternal.

This one thrives on rhyme
and meter—lots of it.
He eats it up for breakfast.

Then he's out the door,
scooter at the ready, no helmet,
just the wind in his ample hair.

I show him photographs
of squashed heads, purple eyes,
brains seeping out across a pavement.

They mean nothing to him.
He's young. He's deathless.
He'll live forever, rainbow, evanescent.

An Open Letter to My Class

I know why some of you won't
ask me for a copy of John Berryman's
Eleven Addresses to the Lord:

because you're afraid it's
"too much work" and then
"it'll ruin my perfectly lovely weekend."

"I appreciate your thoughtfulness," you'll say,
"but really, shouldn't you be more
intent on policing my armadillo prose?"

Of course, others of you are just afraid
if you should read these Berryman gems
you'll have to get serious about religion,

and there goes the party circuit!
There goes the late night venality!
There goes the sweet comforts of agnosticism!

I know one of you really really wants these poems.
You really, really crave these Gorgon words
to crack their way into your stubborn heart—

you want them more than you've even
wanted the golden lurch of carnality,
the push and pull of sweet and sour satisfaction,

but you're reluctant to trade the known of that
for the uncertainties of Berryman's insistence
that if a god does not exist it really should.

So I appeal to that one good solid soul
among the dozen of you vegetating in goodness
week after week in our over-heated classroom

primed by the Administration to simulate hell
so we'll know the pinch of suffering
enough to make us choose divinity

at some point in our hard beginnings,
in our brackish search for meaning,
stumbling idea to idea as we swim

our way to understanding that Jesus guy,
who never made much sense to us
except at Christmas when he came with gifts,

that train you had been lusting after,
or your first vial of White Diamonds
to dab behind your adolescent ears.

So now this Jewish urchin gnaws at your
undergraduate heart, and you hate the pain
of growth to meaning in a meaningless world.

But take the plunge! Jump into the darkness
that the pool in front of you presents!
Risk the ping religion inches through your brain!

Go on! Indulge that urge to Berryman your soul!
Swim where the other dolphins
will not swim! Let the murky waters

dampen the feathers they've grown to love,
the soft feathers of disbelief,
the sneering "no" at any occult mystery!

Berryman beckons, speaks to me of you,
the one who'll brave the terse command
"E-mail me those poems because

I know I can't live without them—
I trust your offer just this once
to dip my heart into the possibility that

life makes sense. I want those poems!
I can't go on another day without them!
If you don't send them, I'll haunt your dreams."

So yes, I'll give them to the one of you,
these sweetest berries of the twentieth-century,
the balm for your post-adolescent soul,

the path out of "I don't know, I don't know"
to the joy that you can really live
beyond yourself in the universe of

ever-expanding acceptance of a power
out there somewhere—or maybe rather
deep in the red folds of your hungry heart.

College Students

Grapefruit? More sensible.
Diamonds? More precious.
Holiness? More desirable.

But I wouldn't trade them
for a heap of lima beans,
not even mixed with gold.

So malleable you'd swear
you were working with play-dough
or the stuff that's used to reconstruct chins.

So optimistic you could tell them
Mars is careening towards the Earth
and they'd still go on dancing.

So futuristic the past stays a mystery
they think not worth the semester
or the weekend or the minute.

My life-blood, my Viaticum,
my Eucharistic Feast, my heartaches,
my wisdom teeth, my dreams, my fate!

Poetry Reading at Notre Dame

for Connie Maher

O gentle lady, close your ancient ears.
This body talk is meant for younger blood,
stud-boys laughing through their bawdy tears,
gamboling in poetic earthy mud.

Subdue your eyes into your purer mind
where sacred thoughts can rearrange a star,
a pattern saints will recognize, designed
for making into good what filth would mar.

The rest of us must risk our sweet-bred souls
tuned in to all these syllables of sin,
hoping against hope this poem will end

before the devil warm us high and low.
To close my ears would be no way to win:
I'd never know how holy you have been.

September, Notre Dame

The flowers on campus softening
their colors for autumn, visitors say
"The tea-roses fade." But they don't really fade.

They soften. Memories fade. Your first cat,
the one named "Cat," fades to a corner
of your aging brain, lost in the dust of years.

But flowers in sweet September air
don't die—they gentle into pink
or cream, each tinged with brown and grey.

Except the zinnia—they stand defiant
to swing their red and purple
at students passing by, as if to say,

"We're here and bound to stay—get used to us."
We tolerate their bold reproach, of course,
because we have no brisk alternative.

At their zinnia-mercy as the days
pass into fall, we're reluctant to accept
their brash objection when we want to fade.

The Zac Poems

for Zac Mundwiller

Prelude

California boy, lost
in the kick of leaves
red, orange, brown,

in Indiana autumn, miles
from his ocean home,
miles from endless sun.

But he's happy with
the snow, the ice,
the wisp of dare,

knowing life swims
in challenges,
golden, bronze, and green.

One

The snow'll come, and you'll find the white
of white a comfort as your silken hair
accepts the crystals heaven-sweet, a joy
outside of sunshine, ocean, summer breeze—

the dalliance of January quite
a risk to California skin, the flare
of ice and zero-at-the-bone, the boy
in you released to automatic please.

Regain the monarchy of yearly yes,
relay the welcome of your welcome smile,
and let the play of grace expand your soul.

What's life or love without the push of guess?
An empty plaza or an endless mile
of wonder at the part without the whole.

Two

An empty room, a table, and two chairs—
that's my idea of eternity—
one chair for you, the other one for me,
an occasional seraph to fetch our tea.

Oh, yes, two cups, enameled, as we share
poetic lines, quaint fraternity
sometimes, and sometimes filial, you see,
and Holy Ghost, yes, yes, that'll be

our endless, hourless, passage into Him
Who guards our privacy, our souls a prayer
beyond the holy, fused, no longer two.

The mystic life (such a gas!) not grim,
unhappy human terms as we share
our molecules in common—Me with You.

Three

The gentleness that rocks inside his brain
amazes me—the universe of nerves
concatenating touch by touch in twos
through crimson red and lowly mystic white.

I want to swim there, navigate his train
of thought as it curves, erects, and swerves
idea to idea, words to choose,
the verbs, the nouns, enlinked to syntax. Right!

But can he even guess intrusion here,
a stranger at the gate with news:
"Transfusion comes! Prepare your lips and tongue!"

Upset and ruffled, tear by suffering tear,
he jerks to consciousness, forced to choose
a way antique and yet forever young.

Four

When darkness prowls and I can't see to see,
the candles tremble, light bulbs flicker off,
then only I remain, uncertain, lost,
a convalescent heading into night.

My soul folds in upon itself to be
a victim of the future. Nothing's soft
and furry. Every taste turns into dust.
All roads turn downward, racing off from light.

But then I think of you in hope and joy.
My own self-worth evaporates as you
move farther deep into my restless heart.

You're close to birth, young man, a sunny boy
exploding into manhood, virtue too,
and angel goodness. In you I resurrect.

Five

The train and he are one, heading to
St. Louis, breasting farm fields, the residue
of melon patches, lines of drying onions,
soy beans ripe for harvest, lavender,

here and there a tractor shredding through
the last remaining corn stalks, honeydew,
and winter wheat shoving green bunions
up through crusting dirt dank as myrrh.

He rests his West Coast head to dream about
the adjectives of life, flashing by
pert towns in Illinois, red and brown.

His brain recedes to memory, no doubt
of purpose, cognizant that every cry
from fear to joy crashes sound by sound.

Six

When I have nothing to write about, I write
because my nothing's something, and my something
is an audience of one—that's you, who
read my words to smile or frown. Tonight

I see your anything becomes, despite
the distance, my something. If it's one thing
that I treasure it's knowing that it's you
who swim your thoughts from nothing to delight

my unhinged soul, crawling into wonder
at your growing ripe to poetry.
Let fluid images unclog your brain,

pull something from the liquid evening's thunder,
an anything from nothing. Our amity
becomes our everything in joy or pain.

Seven

Since hope is the most useless of the three,
I'll drop it, or at least avoid it, summers
in my soul or winters in my heart.
The you of you remains a distant fourth.

Whatever sparked the joy of you in me?
Some passing trickster anxious that his numbers
be fulfilled by nightfall? Ripped apart
by awe, I accepted yet another yoke.

And yet this burden's easy, even light,
the touch of wood around my hoary neck.
You'd think I'd learned by years of winsome pain

the fright of pull, the agony of bite,
but no, it's back again so I'll expect
less harm if I hold back to sing again.

Eight

A candle in the wind, he's primed
for fire, but the breezes never stop
so anxious wrinkles crease his lilied brain
as metaphors leap sideways nerve to nerve.

The question is "Can he wait for time
to calm the storm, let ideas drop
into his words?" He's more than patient, tamed
by virtue, energy, quick to serve.

Let inspiration thrive! That's my prayer
for him, the man of gentle, fragile gifts
for linking nouns and verbs at quiet pace.

The wind will die out soon, but if it dare
return, he'll front it, trading whats for ifs,
his soul invigorated across his face.

Nine

Two thousand miles away I stand and wait,
my heart exploding with desire to sense
your words concatenating sound, the nouns
inside the strength of verbs "I do," "I will."

No one can envy emptiness, my state
by day and night, lost in stars, hence
my lust imploding, linking sound to sound,
each adjective and adverb grounded. Still

you come in baby steps, your ginger hair
enticing light, your eyes on fire, your soul
in amethyst, fingers weaving cherubim.

Not soft, not hard, you swim in air. I dare
to map our coming and your going, my own
desire to touch the ache with seraphim.

Ten

The morning cool with the Christmas tree
unlit, awash in darkness, ornaments
returned to quiet as I finger quick
the lamp to spread the room in hellish light,

the sudden silence as the manger scene
returns the awful silence, kings' adornments
shepherd-soft, when I sing the click
of you become the baby, heavenly sight.

The solemn pine regains solemnity,
the tinsel gone to languor, every bird
unsung, each angel wrapped in mystery.

You may as well be one, propriety
redeeming us, one cherub pert, unheard,
a carol in my brain, fused with history.

Eleven

Alone. He sits with a bag of sullen guts
in biology lab. The would-be doctor
pokes the kidneys, liver, esophagus,
all that's left of a nameless donor.

She thought her gift of life a joy, but
the sloppy afterthoughts in truth would knock her
into revocation, what she left to us
returned to fire and earth later sooner.

Reality is never what it seems—
the drawings in a medical textbook
so clean, precise, so linear, so neat.

This mound of flesh defies his baby dreams
to throw him face to face with truth—he'll look
at blood as blood and flesh as flesh unsweet.

Twelve

If I could bottle up his energy,
I'd market it as cordials in the street.
Labeled as restorative, it'd bring
old fuddy-duddies sparkling back to youth.

They'd dance along in life, a synergy
of tap routines, their geriatric feet
brought down to earthy dirt. And would they sing?
Aria after aria, lip and tooth.

But no, best let them crawl their way to grave,
or after-life would have no easeful charm.
They'd trade their heavenly dreams for instant joy,

their plans gone up as jokes. Better save
the speculation there's a God. No harm
to age and die. How can I tell the boy?

Thirteen

It's over now—the last man to leave
the classroom, the lights shut off, the door closed,
the ancient teacher padding down the corridor,
two gentle ones behind him, talking softly.

The younger of the two confessed no grief
at dancing mind to mind, jeté, exposed
in sunlight from the quad, the tinsel horror
known at parting fallen into scoffing.

Old age and youth—a most unlikely pair—
an archangel, a cherub linked by poems
scattered in the air between the two,

iambics, trochees, imagery, the dare
of metaphor, the touch good-by. Love roams,
religion tamed, refreshed, the me, the you.

Fourteen

Tonight I have an audience of one.
Blithe spirit, take my soul and make it yours.
We fuse in circumstance and love—you there,
me here, two Christmas elves encircling God.

My lord (my Lord!) I'm yours, the only son.
You are my father. I obey, ensured
commands are viral, that you dancing care
these poems can cover message, word for word.

Nativity ensues, you washed in sun,
me Indiana gloom. Removed from you
I tremble in the darkness, lost in space,

the planets whizzing by, one by one.
I wait to be you, vigorous and true,
beginning life, encountering face to face.

Fifteen

To look for Him Who's born this lonesome night
I turn to you emboldened by the thought
of youth, the hair and smile, the hands, the touch
that grace has made minute after minute—

since there inside of you He lives, a bright
too holy presence. I sit in peace, taught
a life of prayer, forgiveness, love, and such,
glad to be at home with your heart in it.

The star is fixed now, shining in its place
above the darkness. You are here within
the crib where angels hover, sing to you,

my God-Man, pure as glass, your sweetened face
my face, your reach my reach, deserted sin
no more as fused we rise in Him—One from two.

Sixteen

As real or unreal as it may sound,
I want to freeze dry his adolescence,
his young adulthood, caught in the fervor
of excitement and his ballet gesture.

So like the sweet amphora that I found
inside an antique mall, its iridescence
overwhelming as I prowled, however
much I quite resisted beauty, vesture.

The pot and he have coalesced to one.
A tense desire to own them both succeeds
in bland frustration. As I thumb the one,

its crispy gold and green resilient, dun
my heart, frustrated as it swims, proceeds
in wonder, holding one into the sun.

Seventeen

Here in the silence of the Christmas tree,
alone in the smothering room of gilt,
of glitter, of rainbow lights, I see a fate
climb slowly down the garland and the branches.

It's the future, and it's come for me,
tired of pretense, holy strife, the still
shimmer of the vows, angelic state,
too good for human stuff, the avalanches

expectation brings to make a man
a god, sinless, perpetual happiness.
If they only knew the inside story,

lust bedeviled, avaricious. Can
a dream evaporate to emptiness?
Witness a solemn end devoid of glory.

Eighteen

The night and I are one. Not out there,
but here, deep inside whatever forms
my soul—harsh at times, unforgiving,
brash, outgoing, restless, nosey, glum.

But then at times you enter me so where
was darkness light seeps in, the gentler harms
of sharing, tense renewal, maneuvering,
and growth, lots of growth—our soul is home.

The secrets of the universe unwrap
their bright-boy toys. We travel off to Mars
for nothing's left us but to see, to know

the click of time unwinding us, the snap
of virtue, polished by the friendly stars.
Brain in brain we'll probe the dark and grow.

Nineteen

Don't try to tame the human heart—it loves
where it will love. Rebuke the wind—it laughs
and spins where it will spin, mussing leaves,
the hair of trees, and fissures in the wall

of moral discontent. Below, above—
who cares where breezes prance and cough their coughs?
Society? Its rules? The ruse of grief
dead-ends, frustrated at its rise and fall.

There's friend with friend—that's it—no rules apply
to love. We watch it grow, water roots,
await to harvest fruit, flesh and bone.

We analyze. We cruise. We watch it die.
It doesn't die. It resurrects in shoots
to search for God together or alone.

Twenty

As a doctor, he'll know the secrets
of the heart: when it skips a beat
he'll sense the truths of chemistry, he'll chart
the rise and fall of close encountering.

I saw him once, a man of no regrets,
take poetry, dissect it clean and neat,
squeeze metaphor, tear simile apart,
then smile in simple pride, a flowering.

He's rather like a daffodil in snow,
caught between reality and promise:
he dances in the cold of wild dreams.

My only luck's to watch him grow,
pentameter at hand, a sweet surprise
jetéing in my life of ifs and seems.

Autumn Lake

The cormorants are gone. I miss
those haughty water-birds, their noses
in the air every evening as I take
my walk around the autumn lake.

They waited for me all summer,
anxious to hold their beaks skyward,
watching me with their black eyes,
making sure I'd note their royalty.

But now they've left, probably
for Mexico where they'll dance fandangos
through the winter, laughing at my
trudging through the snow.

My path knows me well. I can't stop
even if I wanted to because the lake
is mine, take it for what it seems—
birdless, silent, lacking some regality.

Orlando June

When fire in the gut subsides
to ember, and the quiet tears
leave crystal glitter on
the cheekbones, he rises
from the ash-heap remembrance
with a dulling heart made
all too bleak, indifferent to
the suffering of people other
than himself, the swift recorder.

When the newspapers have shifted
his attention to a new frontier
of horror elsewhere on the planet,
and the jury of sweet attractions
lures him to some stasis
in his aching brain, the orioles
newly arrived at their feeder
remind him that sweet beauty
waits just inside tomorrow.

The heavens deal with atrocity
in their own inscrutable way,
and whatever ether-creatures wing
their majestic tracks among us,
he can soon forget the blood,
maternal grief spilling in the heat
where Seminole once patched
their way among the swamp panthers,
the thickened knees of cypress.

Gather him a crown of sycamore leaves
that the North newly sprouts
in mid-June madness under
sun gone viral with humidity
and power, lashing skin to lesions
where virtue once held court
but ceded rights to selfish vigor,
the roller-coaster of emotion
packing locals for their ride.

So put away your banners black
from night-time vigils and rehearse
your souls for repetition since the world
is crazy with contempt but waits somehow
for redemption from a new messiah
promised at the dissolution
of the concrete effigies we build
to watch our feeble tears fall senseless
on the paths to nowhere, nowhere, nowhere.

Reflections on a Trumpet

for David Rowe

His were the lips that shaped the tune
with so little effort you never knew
the acres of pressure the metal endured
from flesh of this innocent Cajun boy.

Far from the bayou, he shared his gift
with goodness so pure you'd swear
an angel of God had slipped inside
the brass phalanx in our school band.

He counted rests the way he courted life—
so softly you'd think he wasn't there—
a chaos webbed into Southern charm
and a smile that rose on command.

If he were ever angry, I never saw a flare
of red, except in Sousa fortissimos
when notes spilled out of him eager
for light and the precision he shaped them into.

Now he's silent, and the joy of his face
haunts every sound from the golden round
hiding the eyes of teenage boys
who have assumed his thrill and made it theirs.

The tubes that curled in his lap between
rides of melody sleep in a velvet case
where hope awaits the ineffable call
that virtue makes to necessity.

The music swims inside of him yet,
and the lure of a song or the whip
of a voluntary or the softened appeal of Taps
will bring him back to his adolescent fare.

Then his filigree fingers will ply the valves,
and his tongue will wet the silver mouthpiece
as embouchure forms and the heavens open
with sound to welcome the living from the dead.

Small Town Lot

Before Little League excavated us,
there was softball in the dusty
schoolyard next to St. Liborius
where the German nuns taught us
rudiments of this and that.

We listened in a glaze of silence,
polite and unexpressive,
but we lived for summer
when the nuns disappeared,
and the dusty lot was left for us.

We aped our favorite players,
chewed and spit like Nellie Fox,
cocked our bat like dark Miñoso,
and we ran to base as if the Nazi
nuns were just around the corner.

Bullies faded at the batter's box
that drew no lines for excellence,
and everyone who rounded for a homer
was an angel in our cheering eyes,
tense for any adulation in July.

So crusty hopes of honor,
winning big-time in the majors,
brought us nightly through our sleep,
ever restless lest the moonlight
interfere with our adolescent dreams.

Puzzle

Why did they strip Bonhoeffer naked
before they marched him to the gallows
that April day in 1945?

Or did he strip himself, wanting
to be as Francis was—naked
in death as he was in birth?

Or did they order him to strip himself,
unwilling themselves to touch
his unsung clerical flesh?

Or did he request to be stripped
like his carpenter-god
so the two could mesh in death?

He declared, after all, it was his birthday,
that glorious April day when he rose
from the dead to his redeemer heaven.

And there he romps, naked and fresh,
beyond the glare of guns,
the hatred of obnoxious war.

The seraphim hardly notice him,
so intent he is to blend into the choir,
alone at last, community.

He turns in the light, eyeless
and noiseless, his triumphant defiance
fused with the wonder of answers.

Rescue

He came to me with zinnias in his hand,
their red so deep you'd swear he'd bled on them.
He pointed to the empty martin house,
no purple swirls circling overhead.

Yes, flowers always grew at his command,
but birds had other plans. He could remember
Aprils when at planting with his spouse
they'd scan the cloudy sky rich with lead,

hoping for some rain to swell the creek,
and forage lumpy garden rocks. Once
a feral guinea pig surprised them, lost

and hungry, cold and damp, awash in squeak.
They wrapped the thing inside a shirt, a hunch
this was their talisman in fur—or so they thought.

When Poets Meet

Can Sharon Olds and Wallace Stevens
have much to say to each other
when they meet in eternity?

He the master of words
and she the mistress of emotion—
how will they meld their minds?

Surely he'll grovel at her feet
even as she rolls her harried eyes
darkened by eternities of abuse.

How he'll wish he had
her touch for the sound of the lash
across her daddy-scarred soul.

And she'll yearn for his vocabulary,
sick as she'll be of confession,
revulsion, remorse, and hate.

What a pair they'll make
flitting among the seraphim,
she avoiding rapture, he avoiding sense.

Oh well, let them battle it out
cloud to cloud, harp to harp—
maybe the Beowulf bard will string by,

stop to referee the incessant bout,
translate Connecticut smirks
for the grubbiness of sex and desire.

Words are, after all, our only tool
to reach another soul.
Whether we chase or hide,

there are the verbs and their cousins,
the formidable nouns, first churned
by Cro-Magnon alive with splendor

at the sound of their grunts bouncing
off the bald mica of cave, the fire
rolling off tongues meant for licking.

Let Sharon and Wallace try their craft
on them! Let them spin their adjectives
past ears that first coined the grunt.

Let Sharon refine them with touch
and Wallace the joy of the peignoir.
Let them wallow around in that!

Meanwhile the rest of us trapped
in flesh will continue to joy
at the game of words words words

as we rip at the bloody flesh
of another kill and trade metaphor,
all in the hope of love.

Spring Rain

for Sally

Falling in gentle tears from somewhere
to drop with quiet noise from the awning
down to the mystic tiles of the back patio

as I sit watching, waiting perhaps for answers,
wondering if the groundhogs will reappear
among the phlox and the early petunias

with their simple scent. Then I think
our life makes meaning out of puzzle,
answers where we've looked at darkness.

Meanwhile he putters around inside
dreaming about the paint he used to spread
in lovely shapes of host and chalice,

white and gold, a touch of black
to accent form, subsiding now
with sweet retirement, our earthly goal

a fresco rich, fulfilled, resplendent.
The angels hear our hymns and wonder
as rain keeps weeping on our patio.

The Green Belt

My friend grows weeds, exotic weeds,
tall, short, fat, round, some thin and sky-bound,
some green, some grey, mean and dangerous,
but fun to touch, to go between their spines
and reach for skin, hard and wrinkly.

The names glide off my tongue:
prickly pear, barrel, horse crippler,
Turk's head, cholla, opuntia, mariposa,
night-blooming cereus (queen-of-the-night),
mammillaria, organ-pipe, claret cup.

Out in the desert they're free, facing the wind and sand.
If grateful for a little rain, they never mention it,
content to soak the sun, channel its energy
to ancient roots, those scraggly threads
anchoring them just barely to the sometime soil.

Paul scoops them into boxes, bounces them home in his car
to prickle his deck and hill. Transplanted into pots
near water (those faces he calls ponds in the grass),
his foreign friends settle into home, make new city pals,
endure his antic nurturing, questing fingers, eager eyes.

Maybe the desert wasn't so great after all.
Maybe the thrill of change is good, once
adjustment turns to sweet compliance.
Their flowers spring to action when we least expect it,
throwing pink, magenta, gold, and blissful white into the air,
along with dusky scents rich, elegant, and sweet.

The Mother

for Andrea

So often she's been sucked with
Anna K into the hungry wheels
of that metal beast

and spit out piece by piece,
you'd never guess this sweet Karenina
was so often eaten by that train.

Redeemed by Grushenka-moments,
she's too busy resurrecting virtue
in the Moscow sluts

to notice men eclipsing her
in the academic marketplace—
she has mouths to suckle.

When her head isn't captive
to a Russian novel,
she's out in the backyard

picking huckleberries,
plopping them one by one
into a rusty bucket.

Her princess-daughter loves them,
preps them for the family pies,
every tenth berry for her princess lips.

The middle child's too wrapped
inside his agile brain
to notice color or the speed of light,

and the infant saint?
It's all "booberries,"
even raisin seeds and paperclips.

What a gaggle of Seattle glee!
And the mountain nestles them,
shrouded by its usual mist.

A Mothered Son

for Damian Dieter, MD

*in memory of
Flora Jean Dieter*

Not afraid of birth or life,
she brought you breathless
into a world of color

where the humor of her smile
amazed you to this day
grey with rain.

You've worked with pain
in others taut with grief,
encouraged them to heal

as she grazed you to laughter,
round boisterous boy full
of happy impish joy,

the way you face your work,
thoughts of her ribboning
through your sutured mind

to swim you through another day,
carrying her inside,
the way she carried you

nine dimple months,
the mother way—
your way, the doctor way.

The New Collector

See the table where he sits
collecting taxes outside the synagogue

under the hot morning sun
as the craftsmen queue to pay their due:

the candle maker drops his waxy coins,
the widow offers up her yearly mite.

One by one they shuffle up to pay,
reluctant or expectant. Either way

they share their well-worn drachmae
so the roads and rulers can thrive another year.

Matthew is their go-between,
the servant of the mighty crown.

Efficient, humble, ready to oblige,
recorder for the government,

he knows the people well,
endures some scorn, shares a laugh.

Then under crisp and cloudless blue
one day a shadow falls across his feet—

the local carpenter stands tall,
pays his tax and catches Matthew's eye.

This day of days is different
as Matthew rises from his perch,

passes records to an underling,
leaves his work and trudges

with a master new and irresistible
out into the countryside, freed of obligation,

open to that call divine:
"Come, follow me." He goes.

Summer School at Michigan

He wrote poetry.
That much I remember.
He told us once poetry doesn't sell.

He said it in class with a kind
of nasty smugness as if he blamed us
for not buying his book.

In class he had a favorite,
an undergrad, handsome of course,
who smoked in the middle of the room.

But what did we care?
His pert insouciance,
his coat and tie every July day.

At some point in that summer
we all stopped trying to answer.
I don't remember why.

But I can guess we all got tired
of trying to read his cramped brain.
We so wanted his attention.

That didn't bother him.
He'd ask a question anyway—
then answer it himself.

He thought that was cute.
We thought it pitiful.
Then the summer ended.

Funny how one man
can transfix himself in your brain,
ache for ache, pain for pain.

Fifty years later
I bought his book of poetry
for one buck on *Amazon*.

Salvation

My friend, a fallen-away Catholic
who never licks his wounds,
told me how nice I was
to visit our mentor Kate
in her final moments
and bring her a rosary.

I told him she requested one,
but that made no difference—
in his mind I was
some kind of a saint
tending to the dying
in their last gasp of air.

So I reversed course and said,
"You're right—I forced my way
into that hospital room,
and I'm going to do the same
for you when you lie in pain
cursing every nun you ever knew.

"I'll pry your arthritic fingers apart
and wedge the coral rosary beads
between your nubby calluses,
and if you ring for the burly nurse,
all three hundred pounds of her,
to get rid of me, I'll scream at her,

"'Step one more foot in this room,
bitch, and I pull out all his IV's—
I'm saving this soul for Jesus!'
And she'll back out slowly
knowing all the candy and roses
will soon be hers anyway."

There's no escaping sin and guilt—
you think you've left the catechism
behind in seventh grade
when you slipped into a public school,
but it all remains, and Raymond
gets it back, right between the eyes.

Twenty Years After

On a sea of hope no deeper than
a Cajun bayou, New Orleans floats,
and images endure:

convicts squatting at the end of a broken
highway, its concrete stump rising
from the murky water

while the ceiling sun boils
as if a hurricane had never visited,
and the nightmare might suddenly fade.

Yet the bodies float by, bags of skin
and rotting flesh bloated by the heat—
they bump into the pilings aimless

as the heart of a city sunk into
its cemeteries on Claiborne, its music
silent but for the shouts of occasional

"Is anybody in there?" through upper floors and attics
from the makeshift barges
navigating watered streets.

The silence stiffens—no birds
because the trees are gone.
Nowhere to roost. No rainbow in the sky,

Just ugly death on holiday,
an early eerie Mardi Gras
along the parade route down to hell.

The hospitals aghast, the airport dumb,
nothing but the not-so-secret cry of Despair
stuttering by the dead, putting pennies on their eyes.

Translations

From the Sanskrit:
Somewhere the moon hides
because the gods are angry,
but life continues
as I move into the forest.

From the Latin of the Sanskrit:
The twice lovely moon hovers
over the mighty Jupiter
while below, fair Rome smiles
into the pine trees beyond the Tiber.
I thank the sacred ones.

From the Danish of the Latin:
The harvest moon hangs / while we dance
our harvest dance / to Wodin, wondrous One.
The mighty men march / as the women plow
next to the fir trees / furled for summer.
The honeyed ale in me / strengthens my sinews.

From the French of the Danish:
Let the moon in her laces come
into my lady's chamber while she prays
to the Virgin, "Protect my lover—
the forest folds danger."
I hear her and smile, my fingers
already on the lute strings.

From the Japanese of the French:
Through trees the moon sees
me, the lady, and the frog.
The lily pad waits.

From the Polish of the Japanese:
Once the moon rises and the wheat
makes noises in the river field,
I push my heavy cart
into the forest and wait for dawn.

From the Vedic of the Polish:
The moon seems afraid,
perhaps of the gods,
but I walk quietly
as usual into the forest.

From the English of the Vedic:
Somewhere the moon hides
because the gods are angry,
but life continues
as I move into the forest.

Virago Intactu

Our literary mag is birthed each spring
like Venus spontaneous from foam.
It appears overnight here and there on campus,
but Sister Angelina smells its coming
and brooms in early to sniff it out.

Peopled with the nudes of *Figure Drawing 101*,
the pages pass between her sweaty thumbs.
The poetry means nothing (she doesn't read it),
but the images of breast and groin and ecstasy
propel her index finger to the phone.

I crouch beside my desk inside the English Office,
ignore the ting-a-ling: I will not answer.
All the blinds are pulled. Summer soon may save me.
Later when I drive away, I see her in the front lawn
of the convent mashing daisies with a power mower.

Wool Gathering

I sneak into Walmart late at night
to feed my latest hobby: crochet.
As luck would have it, the aisle for yarn
is next to *Automotive*. Go figure.

So while the macho men are fingering lug nuts,
I'm loading my arms with skeins of wool:
canary yellow, passion pink, and amethyst.
I stammer loudly: "Damn the little woman—
makin' me buy her friggin' yarn."

Then I scrunch into a side aisle,
weave my way through shampoo, condoms,
and cosmetics, choose a handy check-out,
plunk down my yarn and eye
the short sweet gal behind the counter.

"How pretty," she says.
"I have a thing for color," I volunteer.
She smiles. I decide to bare it:
"I could lie and tell you these are for my wife,
but I don't have a wife."

She giggles, and I go for broke:
"When my mother was alive,
she wouldn't teach me.
She always said, 'Men don't crochet.'
But now she's gone, and I can do whatever I want."

The lady sombers and points a finger up:
"Your mother's there looking down on you."
I clutch my bag of guilt and leave,
heavy again with truth and dare.

Hill Country Heart

In Llano everything's about the river—
no matter where you stand, it doesn't.
The silent mystery of its great deep heart
pounding somewhere under rock
knows what none of us knows:

you can't wait, for everything's going.
Even though the shops and houses cling
to dirt and sand, they're also moving
bit by bit to wherever it is the great rush
of water can and must be flowing.

The people too are running wherever downstream goes,
their spirits trapped in fragile boats.
Some still may think a hundred years of this
or a thousand years of that means permanence,
but they fool only themselves. No sooner

had the ocean disappeared from these dry parts
than the confederacy of pride and stubborn will
promoted the silt of brotherhood,
and the river brought its women to their feet
and gays emerged for baptism,

here where the water washes everything
to quiet witchery, the only noise
the flow of water over rock and the heart
of that mighty, mighty river thumping down
somewhere within the solid blue on granite,

Table of Contents

His Lake 1
The Lady and the Birds 3
Homage to John Malcolm Wallace 4
Abuse 6
Claude/Grief 7
Elegy for Joan 8
Anagama 9
Raku 13
Dirt 14
Satisfaction, as in *I don't Get No* 15
Clifton, Texas 16
Clifton Trailers 18
Clifton Flowers 20
Senior Biology at Clifton High 21
My Clifton Church 22
Alma 23
Trojan Man 25
Her Ground Time Here was Brief 27
In Memory of Gregory Corso 28
What Museums Do for Us 30
The Cubist Game 32
Memories Are Made 33

Annual Torture 35
The Anesthesiologists 37
Candle in the Snow 39
Like Mother, Like Son 40
The End of the Beginning 41
War and Hell 42
Boy 44
The Writer 45
The Pair 46
Outing 47
Country Visit 48
Danseur 49
Taylor Out of Ron 50
The Darker Side of Camelot 51
Photographer 53
The Cellists 54
Glass Blower 55
Ye Olde Rock & Roll 56
The Wreck of the Livonia 58
First Mass 60
A Little World Made Cunningly 61
Brown and Green 62
Grandmother's Kitchen 64
Springerle 65
The Gardener 66
Diamond Wire & Cable, Inc. 67
Mercury Poisoning 68
Aunt Rosella Theodora 69
Great-Aunt Agnes 70
Aunt Tillie 73
Students 75

Hockey Duo 76
Crew 77
Rugby 78
For a Student 80
An Open Letter to My Class 81
College Students 84
Poetry Reading at Notre Dame 85
September, Notre Dame 86
The Zac Poems 87
Autumn Lake 101
Orlando June 102
Reflections on a Trumpet 104
Small Town Lot 106
Puzzle 107
Rescue 108
When Poets Meet 109
Spring Rain 111
The Green Belt 112
The Mother 113
A Mothered Son 115
The New Collector 116
Summer School at Michigan 118
Salvation 120
Twenty Years After 122
Translations 124
Virago Intactu 126
Wool Gathering 127
Hill Country Heart 128
The River and the Man 130

Previously Published Poems

"His Lake" in *Obsidian*

"Raku" in *West Texas Review*

"Twenty" on *Gival Press Web Site*

**Other Poetry Books
by George Klawitter**

Colt

Country Matters

The Agony of Words

Let Orpheus Take Your Hand

His Noble Numbers

Gareth

The Priest

His Lake

It's proximity that shapes us
more than we care to admit.
I know a man-boy, lives

by a lake, brings the lake
with him wherever he goes,
the same quiet depth of water,

the same night creatures
to mumble and slither along
the reedy edges looking for food.

When he walks, he walks
like the lake, sure-footed,
lapping the land cock-sure.

Were there not a fire down
inside his growing soul, I'd swear
he is unknowable, a mystery

begging understanding, no more
a cricket than the angel that protects
whatever lives along, within, above.

If I could lie beside the lake,
I could watch the mystery unfold,
night after night, sometimes

under stars, sometimes
left in the cool of black,
insignificant against the flush

of innocents, able-footed
or finned, skimming the surface,
venturing into the pool,

lost in the wonder of new,
no more a part of understanding
than the broken cattail stems

anchoring the shoreline,
inviting serious study,
quiet repose, agonizing touch,

curious to find the self in water
where the answers lie waiting
for fulfillment, ecstasy, and peace,

dissolution the only finale
worth ample consideration.
So says the sky. So says the lake.

The Lady and the Birds

Instead of working on her novel, she's lugging
fifty-pound sacks of bird seed out of her trunk
into the garage where they'll wait
for her daily scoops. The birds she feeds

incessantly have become her life,
and it's worth the show: the dozen feeders,
the suet balls, the apples on nails,
the ears of corn festooning every tree.

While the blue jays and the cardinals
go about their feast of sunflower seed
and thistle, the squirrels romp
silent for the leavings on the ground.

Least favorite is the roadrunner
who camps ivory-legged all summer and eats
the finches—grabs a finch each noon,
rips it apart, and downs it for his lunch.

Then at night the sweepers come:
the tense raccoons with their ritual washings,
a fox intent on sulky rendezvous,
and a family of naked possum.

They peer into the darkness of her house
and tap the panes to scare the cats
who'd love the chance to go outside
for fricassee of furry this and that.

Meanwhile the grandmother has padded
off to bed to sleep in moonlight
filtering through her avian dreams
where everybody gets along with everybody.

Homage to John Malcolm Wallace

Coon Valley, Wisconsin, a brown October day
when he was propped up at the altar
in a Lutheran church no bigger
than your living room. Mahogany, that box,
closed, of course, against the public he avoided,
and banked with yellow roses.

Away from Chicago, away from books,
his reluctant classroom, and the students
he tolerated with a distant love,
he closed himself away for the last time,
defying us to break his open secrets
or air them in his defiant world.

He knew the sweat of scholarship
and consigned it to a corner
where it belonged in a dusty room,
something to be stroked now and then
in memory of whatever energies
he had as a younger man.

In his silver years he preferred
long summers in the northern wilderness,
close to the Mississippi but far enough away
not to be bothered by it. In a cabin
I imagine comfortable but rude,
he breathed among the wild critters.

He said he'd go to town only once
each summer: to visit K-Mart.
That was it. I don't know what he thought
or what he ate, if anything. Maybe he thrived
on roots and berries. I doubt he had a radio.
I know he had no books or papers.

He existed more than lived,
except for the excitement of hours spent
watching the birds red, yellow, tan,
flitting in the pines and crooning their tunes
to the aging scholar in a wooden chair.
Weeks passed without a human soul.

All the tedious lore he ranged so carefully
in his Chicago office was out of sight.
He joyed among the wrens and whatever
visited his cabin nightly
prowling for scraps or simply there
out of forest curiosity.

Then when he died of city cancer,
they brought him here to a miniscule church.
After a somewhat-service and no talks,
six husky farmers lifted that bulk,
carried it down the steps to the cemetery
off to the right of the stoop.

A bagpiper droned some tunes:
"Amazing Grace" and "Comin' Thru the Rye."
Suddenly a wind from nowhere
swirled down among the autumn leaves,
lifting them in a whirl skyward, then was gone
as suddenly as it appeared. So too John.

Abuse

for Don Cellini

A poet's soul is delicate.
Like spider phlegm it breaks easily,
snapped by an errant bird or deer

or human. Poets spawn their specialty,
spin their meter soft and gentle
when they write of daffodils and spring.

But they have winter in them too,
lash out from time to time
at silly kings and presidents.

No matter. When they sit on lyrics,
nursing tone and phrase, they calm
their anger into line and break.

Here's where they're vulnerable—
exposing thought and sentiment.
That's when they need our praise and wonder.

If I hurt your weaving pen,
if I trampled on your sweet iambics,
I drain my spleen and offer you tercets.

Claude/Grief

I know a Southern boy as sweet
as new spring grass, a smile
as welcome as unexpected rain.

He speaks in gentle lyric syllables,
honey for a warm beignet,
and charms forever May, forever May.

So when he suffers loss,
a brother gone, the hurt is viral.
We feel for the both of them.

But the sun will grow again,
a stronger star, and his face
with crescent joy will spin for us,

the phoenix in him ruff its feathers,
and his heart return to song,
to life, and best of all to us.

Elegy for Joan

A lady of a thousand kindnesses,
she moved in lavender, a soul unknown
to bitterness or gall. She reasoned well
beyond the human, and we sensed in her

a bright angelic draft of sweetnesses
primed for us, her literary zone.
Intelligent, our histories will tell
her grace, her gentle bent to hear and stir

discussions crisp, Marvellian. We are
the richer for her insights and her sweet
response to life. She watched us from inside

a soul with answers, and now she's a star
to shine within our struggling minds, a treat
through plodding study, celestial light beside.

Anagama

for Chris Pate

He robs the forest
first for mud,
then twigs.

The mud he separates
by color, feel,
and smell.

The lumps grow
into mounds
grey, red, and black

around his workshop
gone to dirt,
gone to earth.

The smell becomes
his smell, the lumps
his fingernail friends.

The wheel spins—
fate slips her charm
into his festered brain.

A cup appears
and then a mug, a vase,
the shapes rotund or clipped,

and everywhere a swath
of ridge and rut
projecting from his heart

or rather from the gods
who, using him,
can message us.

And then the twigs,
heaps of broken wood,
splintered for the kiln

where rows of pots
shut in are waiting
for the kiss of fire.

Anagama, anagama,
anagama goes the ritual chant—
anagama, anagama.

Some sparks fly out,
messengers of flame,
swelling from a rant of hell.

You think you control it, but you don't.
Sure, you slung the clay to the whirring wheel,
slipped your watery hands along its growing shaft,

watched it form an embryonic vase
for a final fling with fire
witching from a corner in the kiln.

Cedar branches snap their melody
of crackle this and grumble that
inside the red-hot maw ready for the pot.

Then it's hope, just hope the wood
knows what it's doing as it yearns
for yet another slow attempt at beauty.

Day by day the fire bakes the clay,
the crimson tongues licking at a dish,
blue-green here, gold-grey there.

The muse of fire works her magic
as you sit and dream results
controlled beyond your arty arms.

Then five days pass.
Unearthly quiet settles.
Finally falling light

dies out, the door
unbricked, stone
by sweltered stone.

See, see what fire
and the swarm of gods
created, sweated.

Touch the things
empowered out of nothing
through that dirty Vulcan

who channeled into form
the dictates
of ethereal voices.

Sunlight now,
the mud trans-formed,
the pate exhausted, ecstasied.

We're anagama too, resigned to fate,
embalming choice, ability to shape.
We have no choice, no tough control.

We think we're baking beautiful,
a turn of face, a twist of silky hair
lost in a mist of rabid mirrors,

but cracks in our design, color over crust—
our only choice to marvel at what's done
by gods of heat and goddesses of fire.

Raku

for Shawn Ireland

I'm just beginning to understand
respect for dirt—

how the potter fashions the vase,
molds it shapely under muddy hands,

then leaves it to the mercies of the kiln
to determine texture, color.

In goes a dream, and out
comes fulfillment by the oven-god,

who decides brown or green,
glassy smooth or bumpy rough,

sometimes a combination,
the way life wants to be.

Put the new vase in some company,
next to Roseville or Weller perfection.

Let it sing its primitive song,
there on the table in the sunlight.

Let it croon its craggy way
tough and delicate, a Cro-Magnon chant:

"Touch me. Know my dirt and water.
We came from them, you and I. Raku."

Dirt

What's the truth about an earthen pot
that makes my mind concave and lose itself,
shut out distraction, leave the real world,
withdraw from shape and color, touch and smell?

I raise a piece in awe—as if I'm not
among the living any more. From a shelf
I lift a doyen out of children swirled
with giddy rings of stories it can tell.

It is myself I feel. I run my thumb
around a pert corona, sniff the fire
that fused the bone and muscle, find the thrill

erected out of clay, bid an angel come
in ecstasy, turgid with desire,
forced to merge priapic, will to will.

Satisfaction, as in *I don't Get No*

Since I can't have flowers, I'll take color
in any form of glass, sunlit or not.
Summer or snow, let the green and red fall
into what's left of my heart. The spin of gold,

the royal of amethyst—all the marvel
fired sand can bring I'll take. I've got
them ranged in rows like captive pretty molls
obsessed on self. They primp along the shelf.

The thing about a vase—you know you'll rot
centuries before it crumbles and
its seeds return to riverbank or sea.

You'll be long forgotten while a pot
goes on admired, touched, hand to hand,
oblivious of owner, proud just to be.

Clifton, Texas

A town I've never visited,
but there it is, a blip off 35,
suburb to that Waco place
where Baptists rule in iron fits,

a town with a lady's name,
for a pioneer who roped cattle
and slaughtered her own pigs,
restless in the summer wind,

a town that must have fame
of some kind for somebody,
and a monument or two
to dead Indians or slaves,

a town to come back to,
after a life away in Dallas,
realizing the door is always open,
cornpone coming off the grill,

a town with a water tower
and a preacher or two
hell-bent on saving Texas souls
who wandered off and wandered back,

a town with grass and cactus,
a few stop signs, and dusty children
learning baseball and chores,
eager to please, eager to smile,

a town with dark secrets
that matrons know but keep
zipped up inside their denim hearts,
letting only hints seep out at picnics,

a town where nobody drives off 35
unless they know where they're going,
have someone to care for there,
in aches from cradle to grave.

Clifton Trailers

Squatting silvered donuts, they bake
in the Texas sun screaming against the wind,
rocking when a car passes on the gusty road.
Useless to call them houses, but home

to ragged families proud to be alive
out of the drought. Here and there
a stab of garden, scrawny tomato vines,
a cucumber row, a brush of okra,

the ever present hum of insects battering
the screen doors under the blare of country,
all guitar and twang, all of a summer evening
when the heat gets down to comfortable.

Folks begin to open plastic chairs,
snap the tops off beer cans, yell at kids,
and hunker down to solve the Clifton problems,
the ones that make it out this far

from the heart of town, from the heart
of church and school and grocery store,
problems aching for solutions off tongues
gone bust against the futureless future.

Essie's here and Bobby. Grandma's
in some kitchen swapping recipes.
The universe spins on as clueless as this park
of tense jalopies, home by home.

So if the grander scheme lacks answers,
what can we expect of sweaty things
sprawling in the August smells without
a promise of rain or sweet salvation?

You make do with what you can do
and let the Sister Fates get on with spinning,
measuring, and scissoring. Too bad
they can't see fit to join the poker game tonight.

Clifton Flowers

After perfect winter rain, the colors flow
in Clifton—blue between the railroad ties,
purple on the cemetery hill,
white in pastures edging town.

A silent color drips from laurel trees
and stumbles over mossy brick
throwing youthful smells and faces
past the browns of February.

For weeks Clifton children forget
their anger, and fathers their guns,
as the soft of color seeps in corners
angling through their streets and hearts.

Every citizen loves every other citizen.
Feuds evaporate to golden jasmine,
foes reconciled by sweet verbena,
everyone a bluebonnet to everyone.

that special gift the ocean left for Llano
when it trickled to this blameless river
and the citizens converged to worship,
kill, and love each other on its banks,
those shifting banks of ever shifting change.

The River and the Man

He steps along the river hunting rocks,
aware the river's hunting him. He tries
to leave but can't. He's back again

to clamber over stones and silt
watching for the special something
that the river wants for him.

He thinks sometimes that certain pebbles
lugged to light and heaved into the car
will take him back to Llano once
he's safely home, far from the river,

but he forgets, of course, that the water's
infinite in patience. Though it seems
to change as it rushes to get somewhere,
it's really going nowhere except

into his heart where its granite blue
pounds red, and the green of wonder
in his childness reaches deep

and will not leave him anything
but restless, only restless, ever restless,
for a mighty dream of water, silt, and rock.

Just south of Llano we turn the car
onto a dirt road heading who-knows-where.
Across a metal grid of pipes we bump
into some unfenced field,

hill after hill of color,
blue and orange and lavender—
the wildflowers of Texas watching us
under springtime afternoon sun.

We wade into waves of hue waiting
for an animal or two to break the splendor,
maybe a cow or hare or rattler,
but nothing moves except a breeze.

Paul snaps some photos.
Then we head into town to check
its river bed for ancient rocks,
then antique shops for grandma things.

Nothing remains for me now but a hum
in my brain twenty years later—
bluebonnet, paint-brush, verbena,
a quiet touch when I need a break from snow.

Printed in the USA
CPSIA information can be obtained
at www.ICGtesting.com
CBHW070419180324
5496CB00004B/12

9 798385 212057